Romance Your Finance

Romance Your Finance

Kenneth Ricardo Ford

To order additional copies of this book, contact:
Xlibris Corporation
1-888-795-4274
www.Xlibris.com
Orders@Xlibris.com
125305

Contents

Introduction 7

Chapter 1   . . . Are You Ready To Go
            "All The Way?" 11

Chapter 2   Open Lines Of Communication 21

Chapter 3   Saving . . . Whispering Sweet Nothings..... 27

Chapter 4   Keeping The Thrill Real And Alive........... 37

Chapter 5   Dealing With Debt 41

Chapter 6   The Irs Booty Call 45

Chapter 7   The After Glow.. 47

INTRODUCTION

This book is intended to be utilized as if it were a coach guiding you through the maze of personal financial literacy options available. The romantic parallelism is intended as an extra point of reference. It is ironic that these are two elements of life, romance and finance, that virtually everyone will deal with at some point. Not only do they not have traditional means of practical education, they are almost taboo to talk about even in polite conversation. Too many of us learn about these two important elements of life in a haply, catch as one can type of way. Everyone has had some form of a love life or dreams of having one. Everyone desires to be at least financially stable if not rich. The hope of this book is to illustrate a relationship between love life and financial life so that the reader can be even more inspired to improve their financial literacy, and perhaps spice up their love life too. It is often misquoted in the Bible when people say "money is the root of all evil." It actually states "the love of money." We emphasize the difference between the love of money and the use of money as a tool. We don't discount the importance of money in our everyday lives, therefore, the need for proper management of it, but we want everyone to understand the importance of other qualities in life such as character development, morality, and of course love. In other words, as important as money is, it is not everything. Money is a great tool, but a poor master. This book looks to change mindsets. We want to think that money is not the root of all evil . . . but living in poverty is evil when you can do better.

DEDICATIONS

To God, who delivers me despite me.

My Mother, Bertha C. Ford,
a single mom who did a good job in raising us right.

My Wife, Peggy, more than wife and friend, she's a buddy

And to my Children, Niece and Nephew.

Chapter 1

... ARE YOU READY TO GO "ALL THE WAY?"

Making the commitment

There's wonderment in relationships, especially new relationships, when the excitement is still there. The newness and the adventure of exploring new territory is stimulating and titillating. While the mental, social, character experiences are playing out, the physical attractions are always present. Sooner or later the physical heats up and comes to the forefront. However fleeting at first, it tends to attract more attention in the relationship. Decisions come up as to whether you want to keep it light, unpretentious, and above board. Or, are you going to go all the way? Whether it's that special someone or your finances, going all the way signifies commitment. Nothing on the pages of this book will help you if there is no commitment on your part. In love relationships "going all the way" or the culmination of the relationship is theoretically best when the relationship is in a mature status. With personal finance, the commitment must be made early on, if not up front.

Commitment can mean different things to different people. Commitment is the quality of giving in trust or entrusting. There are some features associated with the concept of commitment that, maybe when identified, may help some of us better deal with this ideal. Commitment is a decisive response. Back in the day the old folks used to talk about "having a made up mind." It's about drawing a line in sand, crossing the line, and not looking back. It says you are no longer leaving it up to chance, but you are making a choice. It is taking the decisive control of a situation, at least as much control as possible and you have decided to consign yourself to that situation or person. You make this commitment because you have belief that the person or situation has a perceived benefit. You are willing to conduct yourself and do what is possible and necessary to achieve the benefits.

Commitment calls for being able to identify with whatever it is that you are committing to. Whether it's that special person or your finances. It is necessary to have identified foundational characteristics that can be built on. Identify your likes and differences. What are the commonalities that are shared in this potential relationship? Are they strong and meaningful enough for both parties? Can they survive the challenges that will present themselves? Identify with why you want to be in this relationship and what can be gained. Focus more on why the relationship rather than the how. Often times when the focus is on the how it tends to make success harder to attain. It assigns a work type drudgery that makes it more of a task than an adventure. Thinking about why you want to build a sound credit history or establish a savings account can be much more inspiring than trying to figure how can I start a budget and stick to it. Why do you want to save money? Why is it a good idea to have an emergency fund? Why is having that great credit score so important?

In addition to being able to identify with what you're committing to, commitment also calls for a level of maturity. Sooner or later we all should advance beyond puppy love into grown up relationships. Most of us were young at one time, void of any real responsibilities and able to rely on others for direction, support, and provision. Commitment to a love interest or to your money situation now calls for adult thinking and decision making. When you become an adult, you put away childish things. Maturity is a process. It takes time for a child to grow into an adult. It is not accomplished in a day. Levels of maturity happen at different times and rates for different people. However, maturity is a requirement. That newborn child has no choice but to grow. We should not accept anything less than a profitable and rewarding growth experience in our romantic lives and with our finances. Growth and maturity are directly associated with learning and applying what is learned. Too many people have avoided the learning experience thinking that what you don't know won't hurt you. WRONG! Knowledge is power. Generations of individuals and families have struggled needlessly due to not having access to some of the simplest financial literacy strategies. While at the same time there are other people who have a financial sixth sense. Wise money management and prudent investing come naturally to them. This is not the norm, especially in today's world of complicated and sophisticated economics. Having degrees is great. However, college regimen is not for everybody, and yet everybody is saddled with the challenge of a certain level of financial responsibility if you are going to reasonably maintain a life and household. When it comes to financial literacy, earnings and wealth creation play significant roles. It is important for a person find their learning zone. What is it that you can be great at and make money doing. When you find it, it benefits people and you can make money doing it, then learn more about it than anyone in their right mind would. Become that expert that people don't mind paying for that particular service or product.

In a similar light, when it comes to romance, nobody wants a dummy. Being well read and up to speed on current events doesn't hurt anyone. Of course, being that expert on a particular topic that is passionate to you can be kind of sexy, too. There is nothing worse than wasting time looking for Mr/Miss Right in all the wrong places. Then when they do come along, they by pass you because you spent so much time partying, carousing and searching that you were unprepared when you needed to be. Commitment also calls for the training of the mind—Self-discipline. This is a tough nut to crack especially in the world of today where so many strongholds of educational, moral, and character standards are eroding. "If it feels good, go for it" is the call today. We live in a "What the Hell" generation. If everybody else has the latest gadget, then I must have it too . . . what the hell the cost and associated expense. Commitment is also marked by an attitude of involvement. This can't be treated like a spectator sport. I was once chatting with one of my early mentors, an elderly gentleman who has since passed on, and I was telling of a business venture I was embarking on while still holding down my regular job. His comment was that if I was still working . . . then I wasn't in business yet. Hmmm. True involvement does cost a little of ourselves. We may have to come out of our comfort zones where life is as pain free and soft as possible. Involvement means having to operate in a different orbit where things are unusual and ambiguous. This can raise the stress level in our lives and in general most facets of society warn against that. The position here is that while convenience and comfort are nice, well managed stress can keep you charged up and in tune with life. We all exist in an environment that can be very dynamic and challenging without notice. We can learn to manage these challenges. Most successful people have learned how to find comfort and strength in the midst of uncertainty. All this leads to the implementation on your part of some hope, a little faith and a venturous spirit. You are not the first to try it and make it. And you won't be the last. It's been said that if you're not living on the edge, then you're taking up too much room. There are tens of thousands who were too lazy or too afraid to try, and they didn't make it. Get involved. Allow yourself the seldom used inspiration of commitment. It is better to have fully lived when you die than to be fully dead and have never lived.

RECONSIDER THE RELATIONSHIP, LEARNING FROM AND YET MOVING PAST THE PAST

We've all dealt with money in our past. Whether you got an allowance as a child, received money as a birthday gift, had a job, performed a service, or just got blessed, most us have had access to money. Very few of us still have that first dollar framed on a wall in our homes. Most of it has come and gone. Just like love relationships, several have come and gone. Some of us still have that first love in a picture frame on the walls of our mind while others gave up that memory long, long ago. If you are going to start a new relationship with personal finance, great. There comes a time when we decide to rethink our own relationship inputs and approaches with a special someone and/or with our money. "It's going to be different this time" we sometimes say in our mind. Take an honest inventory of your history with money. Look at your spending habits and your saving patterns. Most of us have had a dysfunctional relationship or two in our lives. The first step toward getting it turned around is to recognize its existence. The other hard part is acknowledging that the dysfunction in the relationship wasn't all money's fault (or all the other person's). We sometimes have to take a good honest look at the person in the mirror. You may ask yourself questions such as "was I a nag?" "Was I too inwardly concerned and showed little or no compassion for them?" "Did I come on too strong or not strong enough?" "Was I too possessive or too aloof?" We are all human and are prone to make mistakes. It is appalling that for a subject so important to life itself, we in America, can graduate with a high school diploma without ever breeching the subject of personal finance. Whatever the problem(s) or mistake(s) of the past ... get over it! Don't get hung up over it and don't let it hang you up. Deal with the future and forget about the past, even if it was a pretty good past. Be willing to place a personal wager on you and your abilities. Dream big. Learn and grow from every experience. Don't get hung up on what you do or don't do to be rich, but Be something to be rich. Let me repeat, don't just do something, BE something! Don't let embarrassment kill your opportunity to pick up new tips and strategies for better days ahead. Move past the past and don't just get it on, but get on with it. As you embark on this new relational journey, whether it's in romance or finance, come to grips with your differences as two different entities. It is said that men marry hoping she won't change and women marry hoping he will change and usually both are disappointed. Try to recognize and emphasize each other's strengths. Develop and maintain a culture of building each other up. Average people rarely do this. You want to be above average, positive upwardly mobile people, and these are the type of people you want to hang around. Positively reinforcing each other can get harder to do as time goes on. Practice changing up the method and the mode from time to time to keep it fresh. This should be fueled by the positive talk you feed into your own brain regularly. Try to think with the logical side of the brain rather than the emotional side of the heart. There is no one "right" way to handle your relationships. Most books (this one included) and other outside information can guide you, but it is generally up to the individual(s) to creatively apply the information to their particular situation. That can be fun, too. More often than not, when we use that thing between our ears called a brain to think about it and get our creative energies flowing we will come up with a way to apply our strengths AND our challenges to make the perfect relationship. We may find it helps to minimize the distractions. Be more concerned with education rather than entertainment. Stray away from the tabloids and reality shows to that which can educate . . . books. Turn off the TV or the iPod so that our brains can truly focus on the issue at hand.

Take a look at the big picture of your money and love relationship. Learn and understand your individual rights and responsibilities. Inquire about laws that may affect your ownership of income and responsibility for debt. Understanding your individual privileges and liabilities will help your relationship. Are there common law issues to be addressed if you two decide to live together?

Whether its love or money a big part of success, along with the deep belief that you can be successful, is taking a step by step approach toward the realization of your dreams. Love at first sight makes good fodder for novels and made for TV movies. While it is not impossible, most of us will have to or have had to do it the old fashion way. Dating and building relational trust and success over time. There were the ups and downs, the good days and the bad. But generally, as long as you weren't dealing with a whack-o, a good many relationships evolved and turned into something where the challenges could be conquered. The bad things eventually melted away and are forgotten and the good things turned into memories. Two people with compatible goals and like ideas on how to reach them is helpful, but not rigidly necessary. Differences of opinions, methods and ideas also go into making a great relationship better. This is where one party of the couple can excel in an area of the other party's weakness or challenge and vice versa. Differences can be a good thing just as long as civility is a component in the relationship. There should always be the belief that you can work out any situation, together. Even if it takes a bubble bath conference meeting, to work out those areas of stress.

A good first step is to set up a budget. Just the mention of the word budget gets the stomach and other body parts to tightening. Budgeting will be addressed later in this book, but it is important to get a written picture of your personal finances.

Secondly, one may identify goals. Perhaps that dream home, a business idea, or preparing for an early retirement. No matter what your age, make the sky your limit. Dream big. If that's not in your DNA and if you're more laid back . . . the sky is still your limit. The process involved in reaching your goals can charge your spirit and be just about as exhilarating and rewarding as reaching the goal.

Next, make a plan. You've got your goal in mind, now you need to plan the route to get there. As the saying goes "failing to plan is planning to fail." Don't get tricked into thinking you're going to make the big leap and wind up in la-la land. Too many people have put their hopes in the lottery magic. There are few ways to win and millions of ways to lose. Even many big lottery winners, too soon, ended up broke after the dust cleared. If you want true success in your life you are going to have to TAKE ACTION to get to where you want to go. In your strategic or overall plan you'll need to plan some small or tactical steps to get you along the way. When you meet those short term goals . . . celebrate! Go ahead and make a big deal out of it and enjoy your small victories as well as the big ones.

Now with a budget, goals and a plan the only thing left to do is DO IT. I know it was just written a few words ago, but I re-emphasize . . .

Take action, execute, put in play, push it, go, start, make it happen, just do it. This is the point that usually stumps people who are diligent enough to get past the first three premises. Try to stick with your plan as best you can.

How Do You Stick With It?

1.)   Daily Feeds. It is very important to feed your mind with positives on a daily basis. Many of us have been bombarded with a life time of negative messages and images. Now is the time to counter with the positive.

2.)   Acquire a Partner for Accountability and Inspiration

3.), 4.), 5.) Add three more of your ideas that work for you_____

Keep an eye toward adjustments as needed. Success is within your grasp.

Chapter 2

OPEN LINES OF COMMUNICATION

Communication is the bedrock of most relationships. If you're in business, there are sales and staff meetings; if you're religious, there's prayer; if you're one of today's youth, there's texting. The point is that communicating is an important factor in relationship building and relationship maintenance. The fact is that even the lack of communication communicates a message. Talking about money and finance does not seem like the type of conversation that would be prevalent in a new budding relationship. Money is an important facet of the relationship! After all, from the first date on, money is usually being utilized. Talking about it might not be a bad idea, if nothing else but to see the other's reaction to such a sensitive subject. We, with the help of Money Management International, are offering some conversation starters to help you "test the waters" in romancing and financing.

- 56% of people who are unhappily married report financial problems are to blame.
- 68% of women place high value on common values and interests in a relationship compared to 53% of men.
- Job security is considered the most important financial trait in a relationship and is valued more than low debt levels, adequate savings, and a good credit history. Interestingly, job security is the one trait of the four that can't be personally controlled.
- Looks do matter. Americans' attitudes on looks appear to be more important than money in a relationship. Nearly half of Americans cite attractiveness as important in a relationship, only a third think adequate savings count. 27% of men say attractiveness is important compared to 18% of women.
- Women may be the most savvy when it comes to financial management. Significantly more women, especially those 35 and older, place a high importance on the four financial measures (job security, low debt level, good credit history, and adequate savings) compared to men or younger people.

Communicating with your money— Telling your money what to do . . .

A Budget / Spending Plan

Sitting and talking to your money giving it a pep talk may not be the most rational thing you can do whether publicly or privately. However there is a way to tell your money what to do. It is called a budget. Some may call it a spending plan. Whatever you call it, it is a rational way that can be learned and adapted to your particular persona, to tell your money what to do (or not to do). Some people really feel special when someone sends a card or writes a love letter to them. It seems to put a special emphasis on the relationship. Your feelings are documented as evidence of the special relational intentions. You can look at a budget in a similar light. Send your finances a love letter. One of my former church pastors always told us to "write it down." Studies have proven that people with written goals or budgets are significantly more successful than people who can simply state their ideas or good intentions. Send your money a love letter in the form of a written budget or plan that indicates just where we are taking this relationship and the steps we're taking to get there.

What does a budget do?

1. It helps get control of your finances
2. It helps keep you out of financial trouble.
3. It helps you to set and achieve financial goals.
4. It helps you become a smarter consumer.
5. It can pave the way to a secure future.

What goes into making a budget?

- Income . . . Your income is the amount of money you are taking in. There are various sources of income such as wages from your job, a pension, settlement payments, royalties, or even alimony and child support. Most people have little trouble recognizing what their income is. Most people don't have a money problem. They have a money management problem.
- Expenses . . . Expenses are the monies that are going out. Whether to pay bills, acquire things, meet a goal or make some kind of move, virtually everything that takes a piece out of your income is an expense.

  - Fixed Expenses (rent/mortgage, car payment, insurance, internet, etc.)
  - Variable Expenses (food, utilities, gas, entertainment, etc.)

The only way to know exactly what you spend is to track your expenditures. Do you know where your money goes? Most people can tell you house payment, car payment, utilities or food, but after that, things can begin to get a bit fuzzy as to where the rest of it goes. This is usually the best place to begin putting together your budget. Start tracking your spending. There are a number of simple and creative ways to track your spending. The important thing is to adopt one today, and get started. The simplest method to track your expenses is to get one of those little note books at the dollar store. Now set aside a period of time you want to track. A day is fine, but a week or two would really help to emphasize what you're really doing with your money. And track <u>EVERYTHING</u>! No matter how small or insignificant it seems, write it down. Doesn't matter if it's the candy bar you bought on impulse, the donut and coffee you got on the way to work or the dry cleaning you picked up on the way home, write it down. In doing this, you are also practicing the development of self-disciplining skills you are going to need.

In your love life you'd need to clear it with your significant other before you go nagging, I mean digging and tracking into their lives. Keeping track of your time individually, their time individually and your time together may be nice and help to build memories and milestones in the relationship.

Credit Reports and Credit Score

We are generally taught to not make judgments against people. Most of us don't care for being judged either. However, in the real world, people are making judgments about others on a regular basis. Everyone wants to know "what you're working with." We all want to look things over so we can get an idea of the score. Whether you're a man that snatches a peek under her short skirt or a woman that steals a glance at his crouch, human nature has a desire to view those unmentionables. Credit reports and credit scores should be no different. We all need to do whatever it takes to view these private parts in order to avail ourselves of any potential surprises.

There are several reasons to check your credit report.

1. Make sure there are no mistakes that could hurt your credit
2. Track your history of payments
3. Protect against potential identity theft
4. Keep your inquiries to a minimum
5. Stay on top of your credit without hurting your credit score.

Everyone is entitled to one free per year from each of the three credit bureaus. Go the www.annualcreditreport. com to get yours. The three bureaus are Experion, Equifax and Transunion.

Chapter 3

SAVING . . .

WHISPERING SWEET NOTHINGS

Saving is more about creating new habits and looking at your money in new ways. A lot of it is trusting your instincts and using common sense. When it comes to saving there are two types of people-those who save and those who wish they were saving. Which are you? In today's fast paced world people get bored easily with the simple pleasures of life. The concept of saving usually conjures up many mythical apparitions. It is sometimes hard to see saving when it seems like every dime you get seems to be needed for something. If our lives aren't electronically charged with intelligent technology at the speed of light, then what's the point? Is it possible to forge a deep interpersonal relationship with another human being based on time together experiencing each other, eye to eye, mind to mind, creatively, and at low or no cost?

We think, yes. Whisper sweet words about the nothings we can do except sit and enjoy each other's presence. There is power in quiet time. It allows one to collect and center themselves. The same is true for couples being able to build a relational foundation from within instead of one built on outside entertainment and influences. If you start needing these outside forces to make your relationship, then in order to stay together, those outside mediums must get more and more stimulating. A good mix of the two, quiet and the exciting, can usually benefit you both. Maybe you can operate on spur of the moment inspiration or you're the type that likes to plan down to the "T," we'd like to offer some ideas on inexpensive gifts and activities that can prove priceless to a relationship:

1. Write a love letter or a poem to your boo. This one of a kind gift is not only inexpensive but it also designs a special place on earth for YOUR relationship. This is a great opportunity to let your creativity shine not only from the mind, but also the heart.
2. Prepare a romantic candlelight dinner. In the privacy of your own dining area, create the atmosphere and ambiance of a four-star restaurant for two.
3. Treat your loved one to a personal spa treatment. Give your boo a foot and back massage in a romantic atmosphere with candles, incense, scented body oils, bubble bath and well, you get the picture.
4. Breakfast in bed is always a nice touch.

5. Give your lover a break. If you usually divide the chores around the house, give your partner a break by doing both your shares. Giving them the opportunity to relax and store up extra energy so they can show you how much they appreciate you appreciating them!

6. Create a sound track of your romance. Choose songs that are meaningful for the two of you.

7. Dance night. Turn your living or family room into a night club for two. Have your kind of music, your kind of libations, dress the way you want to, and act it out in the safe acceptance of each other's company.

8. Rent movies instead of going out to an insensitive movie house. Pop your own popcorn (which can be had at a significantly more reasonable price), enjoy your favorite beverage, and snuggle to your heart's content.

As important as saving is, earning power is even better. Saving is a moot issue if you are not earning something to save. It is important to save enough so that you are able to take investment risks in order to increase your earnings. Risks are not to be taken lightly. Learn what you're doing before you take risks. Losing sometimes in an investment does happen. Be encouraged that as you learn you will be able to earn more, again, most people don't have a money problem, they have a money management problem.

Living below Your Means or the art of self-gratification

We've all heard that we're not supposed to keep up with the Joneses. We are often unaware of the debt or financial stress that is involved in supporting the Joneses lifestyle. Instead of comparing ourselves to what we think others are doing, it is more prosperous to cultivate an attitude of gratitude. Looking at and appreciating what you have instead of what you want to have should be inspiring. After all, the poorest people in America are still richer than 9/10ths of the world's population. Setting priorities in our lives is crucial. Realizing the difference between our wants and our needs is critical toward establishing and achieving solid financial goals. In order to achieve certain goals or make adjustments for economic downturns, we may have to cut back or do without. This relates to finance and romance. You may desire filet mignon but have to settle for tuna fish. Or you may desire to be with Halle Berry but have to settle for choked chicken. Or day spa treatment dreams may dissolve into a few jogs around the block and a hot bath experience riding the monkey bar. While on the subject of "choking your chicken" or riding the "monkey bar" (using a vibrator), self-gratification can go deeper than it would seem on the surface. We can all use a little extra special help from time to time. With our finances we may need to use financial counseling or coaching. We may need to put into play some outside objective influence that specializes in the one area that needs it. Surveys indicate that over one third of women own a vibrator. That instrument, just like a personal finance counselor has one main task or focus. They don't get emotionally involved before or after. Men are most likely to reject these forms of "intrusion" into the personal lives of a couple. Men can feel threatened of their position as the king in these areas and become wary that he may be replaced. Yes, there are some great male money managers out there. If and when couples are having money problems in the relationship, indications are that women are more likely to seek outside help than men. By and large women have been strangely positioned as better money managers. In similar fashion, women's most sensitive sexual spot has been strangely position for less than maximum benefit in normal sex between a man and a woman. Some couples may agree that these forms of extra-relational coaching by use of a vibrator may work for them. It is safe to say when men can get over the pride, whether you decide to use a financial coach or a bedroom coach, when mama's happy . . . everybody is happy.

We sometimes must "make do" for now in preparation for better days ahead. Some of the needed self-control or disciplines for making better financial decisions will be covered later. We will offer some tips on simplifying your lifestyle, cutting expenses, and perhaps even finding money to save.

- Opt out on email sales alerts. Electronic junk mail may not be as cumbersome on the environment, but can still tempt you to spend money on things you don't need.
- Take advantage of your bank's free tools. Use these free online tools to track your spending to see where your money is going and where you can cut back.

- Watch TV for free. The research may be a little daunting, and there may be some start-up cost involved, but the long range savings can be significant. Check out Hulu.com and network websites.
- Travel for free. Take advantage of credit card reward programs and airline mileage.
- Eat out less often. Learning to be a better cook can save money in multiple ways. Cheaper preparation cost and cooking in larger proportions to create multi meal left-overs are a couple of the benefits.
- Are there alternatives to that gym membership? Check thrift stores or Craig's list for deep discounted used equipment.

Saving money sets you up for other advantages in life such as

- * Desire for comfortable retirement *Living your dreams
- * Prepared for the unexpected *Building real character
- * That free/independent lifestyle *Prepared for any opportunity
- * It just plain feels good

The best advice for living below your means is to do what it takes to raise your income level to the point that your needs and many of your wants can be managed for less than what you make. That is a simple statement to make but, can it become real in my life? Change your mind set to that of a rich person's. How much would being called a snob really hurt you? Especially when it's coming from people that envy you. How much would it bother you to not have to make a choice between family time and earning a living. Being well to do can eliminate that dilemma and you can enjoy the best of having it all. Financial literacy can open these doors for you, but it doesn't come easy.

Self-Control/Self Discipline

The words on these pages or the best of intentions are worthless without the self-discipline to implement what you're reading. Self-control or self-discipline are two different names for the same thing. It is the ability to control one's emotions, behavior and desires in order to obtain some reward, or avoid some punishment later. It takes a measure of courage, faith, wisdom, knowledge, and strength to employ the self-control and discipline that increases your chances for personal financial and relational success. Self-discipline is usually gained in a process of time and rigorous attention to the task. In a recent conversation with a friend who was recalling his early days in boot camp. He remarked how they were rigorously admonished to wipe away many past ways of doing things and fastidiously attend to all the new things they were learning. They were being taught discipline and structure which most young men could always improve upon at that age. Self-discipline/control is usually best learned when administered by outside forces. It is not impossible for one to train themselves and self-effectuate this element into their id. However, the majority of us learn this better and quicker when held accountable by entities other than ourselves.

How to attain and maintain these qualities would take a book dedicated to the subject itself. The steps outlined here can help one get started on a right path toward developing self-control. There are other books and programs purely dedicated to this topic.

1. First identify what areas of your life you need to gain more self-control. This book is dedicated to financial issues, but perhaps you lack self-control such areas as eating, work, shopping, sex, exercising, gambling, drinking, smoking, or some other obsessive behavior.
2. Try to identify the emotions that drive you to that area of lack of control. Is it anger or pleasure, resentment or fear, unhappiness or dissatisfaction?
3. Give yourself a pep talk several times a day, every day. Deciding to go through this and sticking to it the first month is critical. You may periodically change up the pep talk to keep it fresh or it may stay the same for that month if it works for you. Your talk or mantra may include such items as : telling yourself that you are in full control of yourself, tell yourself you have the power to choose your thoughts, emotions, and actions; Tell yourself how self-control gives you inner strength that can lead to success; tell yourself that you are in control of your reactions; tell yourself that you are in charge of your behavior; tell yourself that day by day your ability to control your feelings and thoughts is increasing; tell yourself you are gaining control of your emotions; tell yourself that you are the master of your life; and finally tell yourself that self-control is not only fun and pleasurable, it is also profitable and peaceful.

4. Visualize yourself acting with self-control. See yourself taking care of business calmly and with self-mastery.

Addicted To Love . . .

One very real drain on a person's economic success is to be caught up in a habit or addiction that is costly and degrading. An insidiously sinister malady overtaking and overwhelming alarming numbers of good people is the get rich quick syndrome. Earlier mention was given to the "lottery magic." With the number of states operating lotteries and the number of casinos open or being opened, the market for this particular outlet is on the upswing. Years of reading has exposed me to one concept called temperance. Temperance or moderation in all things is desirable and to allow anything to completely consume your psyche and time is detrimental. The aim of this book is not to bash the gaming industry because addictions can come in many forms. Sure there are gambling and drug addictions. A person can also get caught up in too much food, shopping or television. Maybe one has let a significant other hold too much power in their relationship. Perhaps video games, facebook, sex, drinking, money, or the pursuit of power have taken an unnatural proportion of your time and space.

These activities not only drain your fiscal resources, they've also been shown to diminish character. Most people who have this problem are not aware of it or not accepting of the fact that they have it. In addition, they think they can quit anytime they want to. The steps outlined in the section about self-control can also be used to help combat this type of problem. Getting other forms of help is also encouraged.

Chapter 4

KEEPING THE THRILL REAL AND ALIVE

The Credit Score

Every life and every relationship goes through ups and downs. Keeping the freshness and thrill can be challenging and yet fun. Occasionally, turning your challenges or to-do-lists into a game can make the performance more palatable, easier, and fun. Doing this in no way diminishes the importance of the job or relationship, but life is sometimes called a game. Many times in business using savvy or making prudent business decisions is called "playing the game." Putting a gamelike mindset to a task or even the maintenance of relationships can take the drudgery and the "work" aspect out of it and add some spark to what needs to be done, and as with most games it is relevant to keep score. Keeping the freshness and thrill can be challenging and yet fun. It can take work and a certain intentional focus, but the rewards can be priceless. But who's keeping score, anyway? Well, like it or not your lover is keeping score, the credit people are keeping a score, and to be honest, you are probably keeping a score on your partner, too. In a perfect world we should get along doing our level best to support, give comfort and stimulate each other. However, it's amazing that when money gets tight, there are cut backs on the job, things are breaking down, everybody needs shoes; the lack luster bedroom performance on this date, that time, and this other time, seems to make its way into the conversation. Yes scoring systems are in place and they are up and running. The financial world keeps score with what is called the FICO credit score. Credit scoring is set up in this rating system:

750+	Your credit is excellent. You can get higher credit limits limit and qualify for any loan
600+	You are responsible and credit worthy
600 or below	Less than perfect. Have had bumps in the Road
550 or below	Difficult to obtain credit.

FICO is an acronym for Fair Isaac Company. Another system that provides credit scores is called VantageScore. The FICO system tracks one's credit report information and uses a formula to determine the credit score. The formula takes into account payment history (35%), amounts owed (30%), the length of one's credit history (15%), how much new credit is involved (10%), and the types of credit used (10%). This information is assembled and formulated to form your credit score.

Your credit score changes constantly in response to your credit activity. Depending on what the activity was determines whether your score goes up or down. A high number of credit accounts with existing balances that are on your credit report can have a negative effect on your credit score. Also, keep in mind that credit accounts on your credit report that are close to your credit limit or have reached your credit limit can negatively impact your credit score. Some tips that may help you to keep from having negative impact on your credit score include:

- Try to keep credit card balances to less than 30% of credit limit
- Limit accounts that carry a monthly balance
- New loans can temporarily lower your credit score
- Don't open new credit accounts if you don't need them

Storing up in the good times, whether it be memories or money, helps to ensure something is there to fall back on if needed. The concept of saving usually conjures up so many mythical apparitions. It is sometimes hard to see saving when it seems like every dime you get seems to be needed for something. When times are good we sometimes don't see the need for saving. In love it is good to get those "brownie points." Those "Ahh, yes" moments are precious and should be relished and saved up. Like repeated bank withdrawals quickly deplete not only the principle amount but also the potential interest that could have been gained. It only takes one "Aww, shoot" moment to wipe out a bunch of "Ahh, yeses!"

The same applies with your credit score. The more responsible you are in doing the accepted norms, the better your score will be. Remember though, it really doesn't take a lot of "mess ups" to put a negative slant on your score.

Chapter 5

DEALING WITH DEBT

In all relationships, we should practice doing the right thing. If you decided to meet for dinner at 6:30 then do that. If tonight is the night for cuddling and a movie, then keep your word. It's the same if you created a debt and promised to pay, you should pay it. There are times, however, when unforeseen circumstances pop-up that make it difficult or impossible to keep your agreement. To become debt free is not only a possibility; it should be a priority-for everyone. Some signals that you are in the debt danger zone:

- You pay only the minimum amount due each month
- Your total debt balances rarely shrink
- You take out new loans to pay off other loans
- Skipping payments

- Buying items on credit where you once only used cash
- Past-due notices
- Collection agency calls or letters
- You get turned down for credit

If you find yourself paying unnecessary late fees or unable to locate statements, the simple and under used solution is to organize your bills. We again go back to some of the already discussed basics concerning self-discipline and writing things down. Try to organize your credit card statements and other bills as soon as you receive them in a file drawer, file folder or other safe place that you will remember. Use a reminder system such as marking a calendar or posting notes to yourself, to ensure that your bills are paid on time. Establishing a system for organizing your bills can help prevent you from losing track of your statements and thereby save you time and money. "But," you say, "I know what I have to do, I just don't have the money to do it." If you can't pay your bills then you should:

- Talk with your creditors . . . "there are many reasons for not paying your debts; however, there is no reason for not communicating with your creditor(s). Contact creditors before bills are due. Explain your situation and the reason you cannot pay. Inform them of you current income and possibility of future income. Let them know about other debts you have. Indicate your plans to bring the debt up-to-date or offer to negotiate repayment terms.
- Set up a plan to repay

- You may consider a consolidation loan or, as a last resort, bankruptcy
- Consider a financial counselor

Five things you can do to reduce debt are:

1. Decrease Your Spending
2. Understand Your Debt
3. Goal Setting
4. Pay More Than The Minimum
5. Tracking and Budgeting

If you find yourself in a hole, the first remedy is to stop digging. Cut back on spending, stop borrowing, and make a plan. "The difference between a setback and a failure is one thing—your attitude."

Remember that debt collectors have rules of ethics that they must adhere to. The federal government instituted the FAIR DEBT COLLECTION PRACTICES ACT to help protect consumers. The job of debt collectors is to get you to pay and many have gone beyond certain limits to do so. One tactic is to stress you out and take you emotionally out of your game, so stay calm when talking to them. Federal laws limit them from calling before 8:00 a.m. or after 9:00 p.m.

Chapter 6

THE IRS BOOTY CALL

Culmination of the relationship . . . Taxes

We've all heard the saying about the inevitability of death and taxes. Tax is like the orgasm of personal finance. After April 15th the nation rolls over and gives out a collective sigh of relief. All the foreplay activities of getting an education or skill acquisition, showing up every day on the job so that you can get that paycheck and everything thereby associated leads up to the heavy petting of filing your taxes to reach that moment of release on tax day. Some can pay their taxes in a premature manner, but everyone is different. Whether that experience on tax day is not what you would have liked, just so-so, or great we have that feeling of "Whew" when it's over. Everyone's tax situation is different and we are all responsible for paying what is legally due. We are also responsible for making sure that we don't pay more than is legally due unless we choose to.

If you have a tax bill, this takes precedent over all other bills (save maybe your house note). Emphasis on maybe.

Ideally, we should start planning our taxes on April 16th. Keeping a good record system and educating yourself to your applicable tax laws could help save money and heartache in the long run. This may save you from an IRS booty call.

Chapter 7

THE AFTER GLOW

In movies, the after math of a couple's intimacy was usually marked by the smoking of a cigarette. In real life there is sometimes the tendency to cuddle or embrace. Still there are others who fall dead asleep while another might jump right up and continue with life's business as usual without even a glance back. The point of stress here is the cuddling in the afterglow. The act of continuing to give and take affections.

Likewise in your personal finance life, after you've worked hard, received your pay, taken care of business and paid your taxes, there's still another possible phase. Giving. Whether its tithes to your church or helping out with many of the worthy charitable organizations. It's been proven over and over that the best way to real wealth is to give some of it away. The majority of our major corporations have discovered this secret. That is why most of them have established philanthropic divisions in their corporate structure. The message here is not about cuddling with your money but trusting enough that you will let it go that it might return to you later. Of course it works better when your motives for giving are genuine and you are not really expecting it back. This is one of life's strangest paradoxes. No one can explain why and how it works. It just does. The beautiful thing is that once you embrace and give to the less fortunate, the rewards are so deep they also defy explanation.

As said in the introduction money is a great tool, but a poor master. There are so many other facets that go into making a well-rounded individual. Character, integrity, spiritual development, intellectual growth, and physical health are some of the other elements. With a good partner the two of you can mutually assist each other in the attainment of these facets with encouragement, fellowship, and accountability. If it so happens that you two like each other's intimate company and can make money too, then you've really found the key to ROMANCE YOUR FINANCE.